Can You Touch Your Nose?

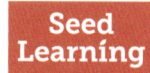

eye

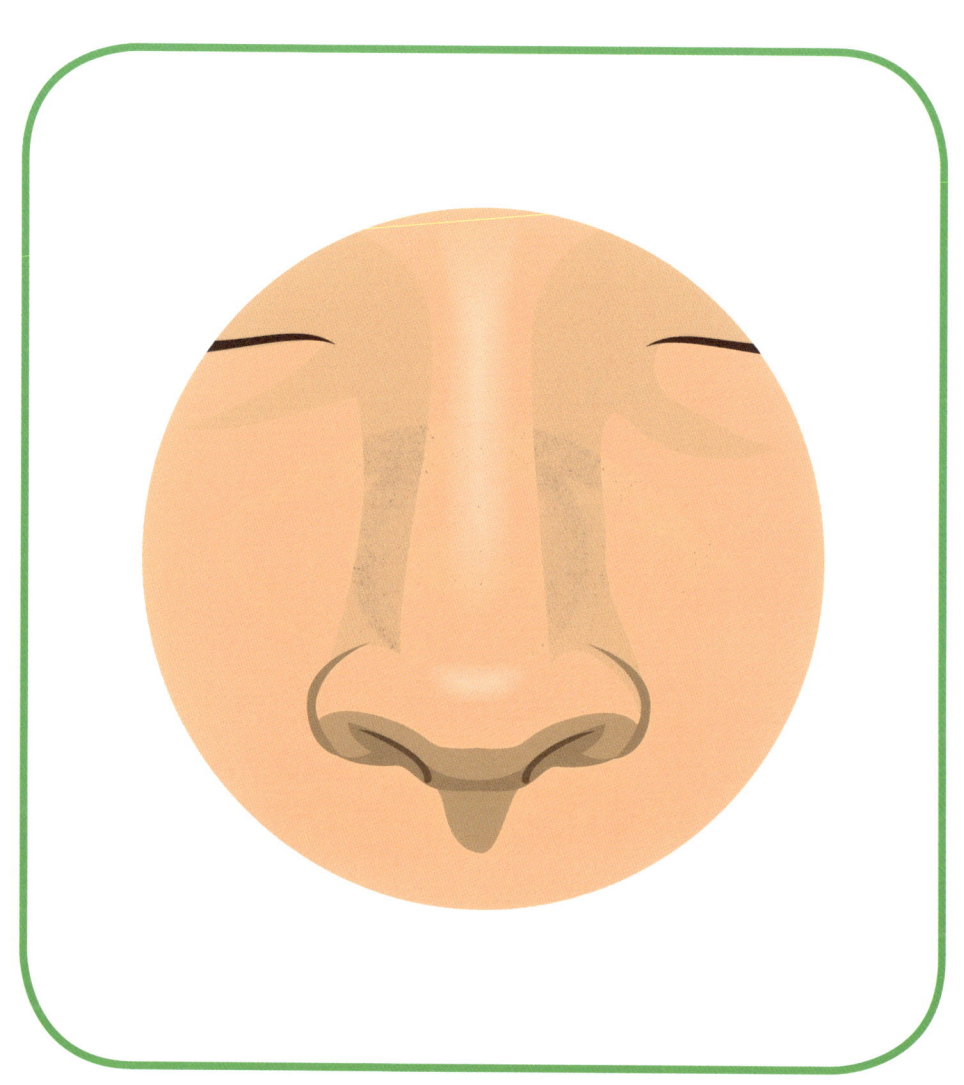

nose

mouth

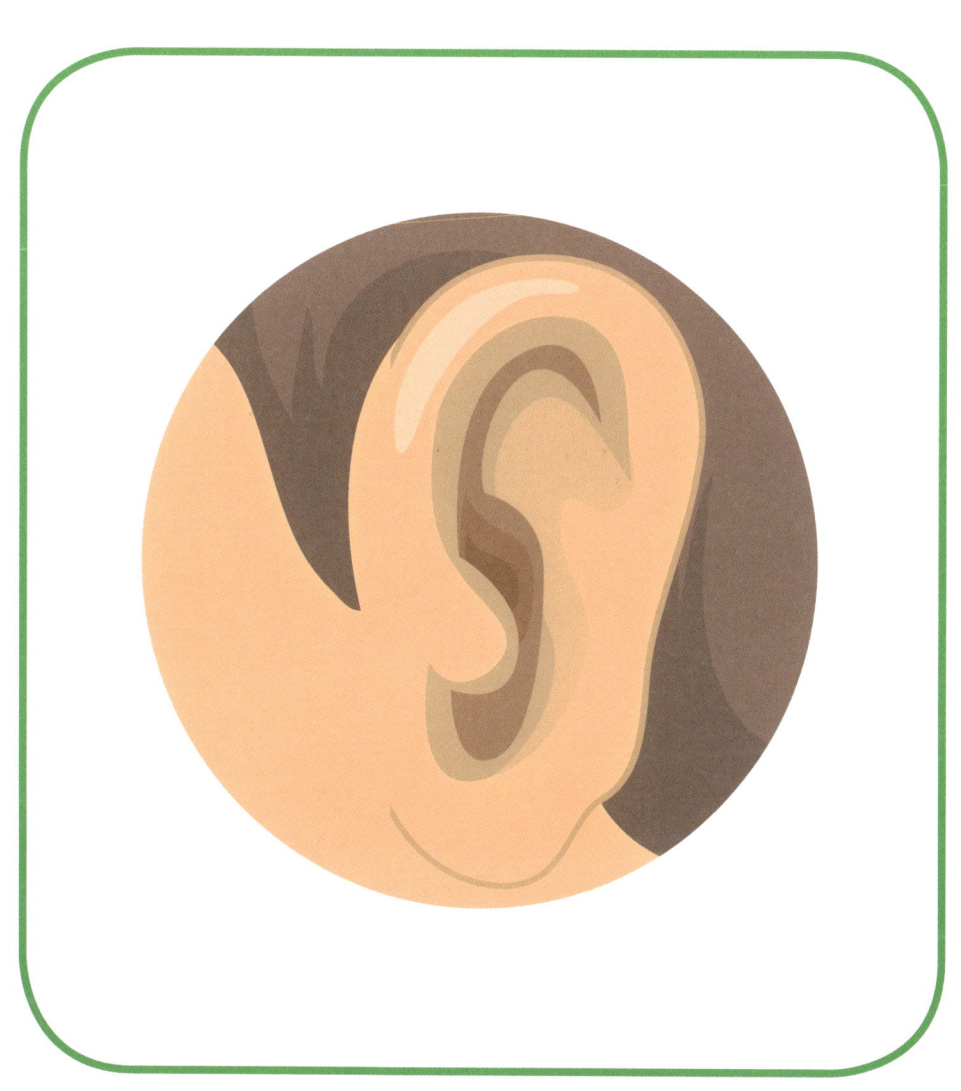

ear

head

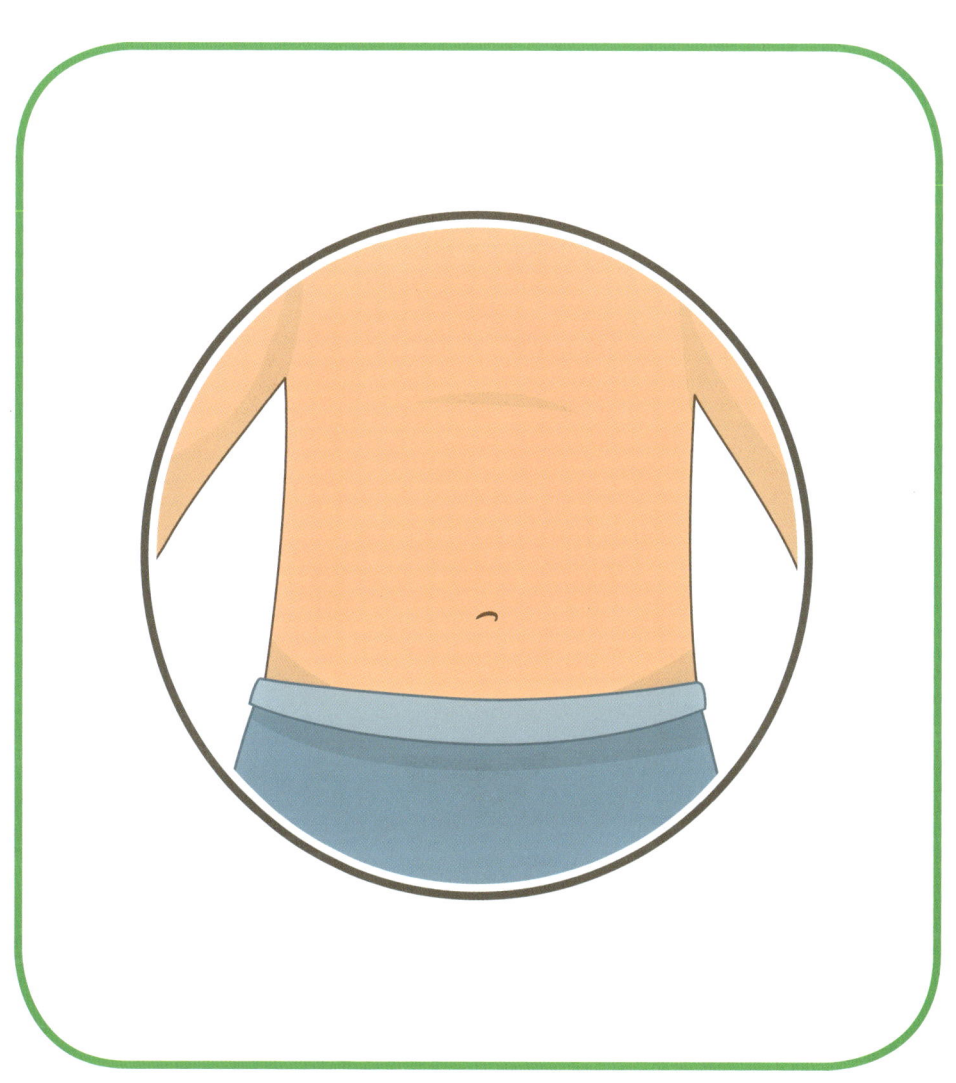

tummy

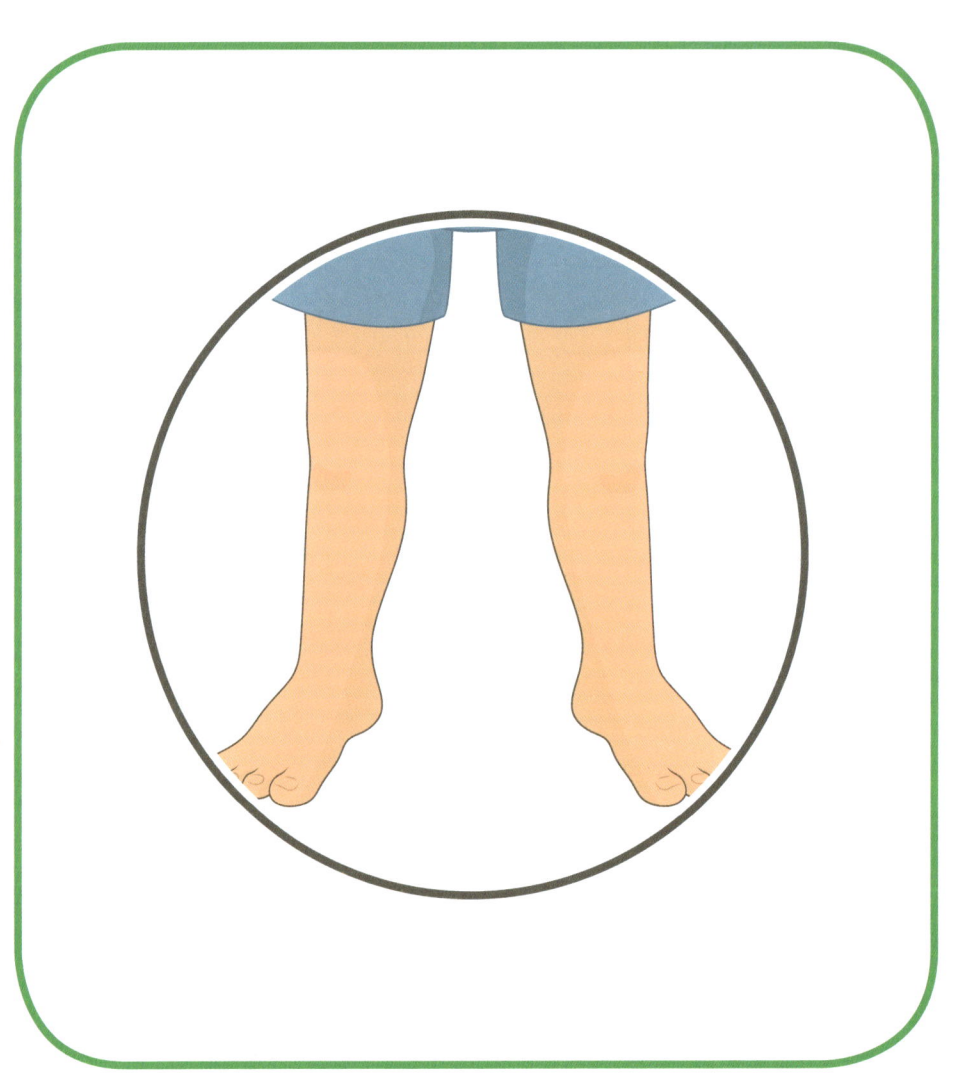

legs

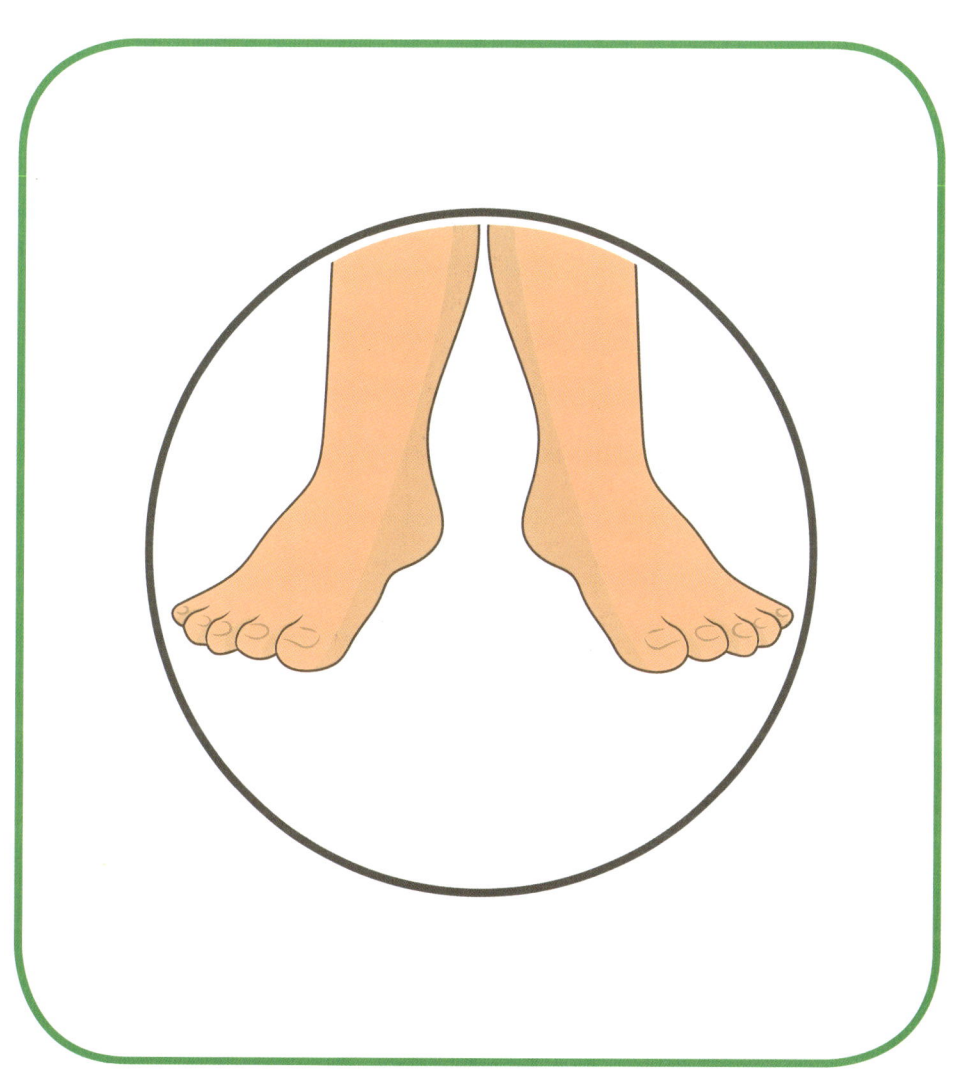

toes

Can you touch
your nose?

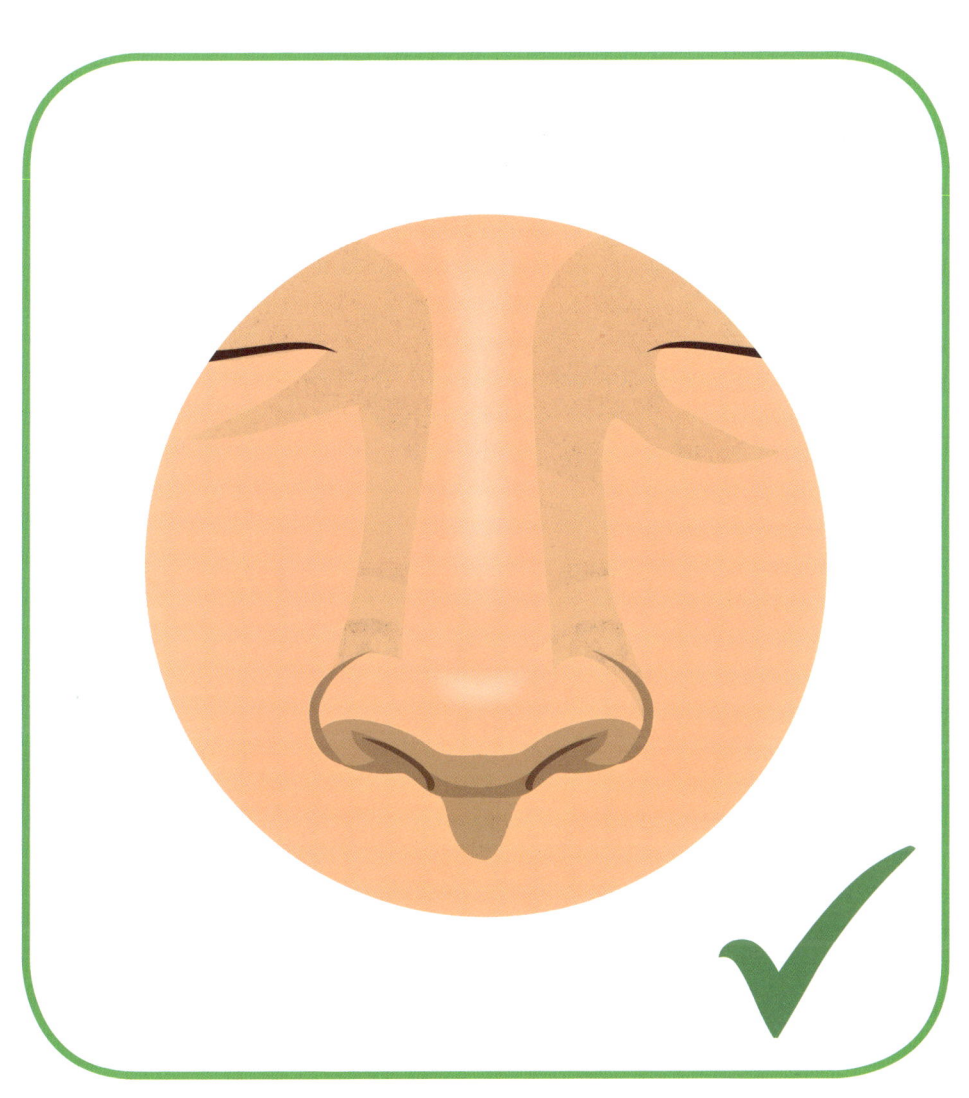

Yes, I can.

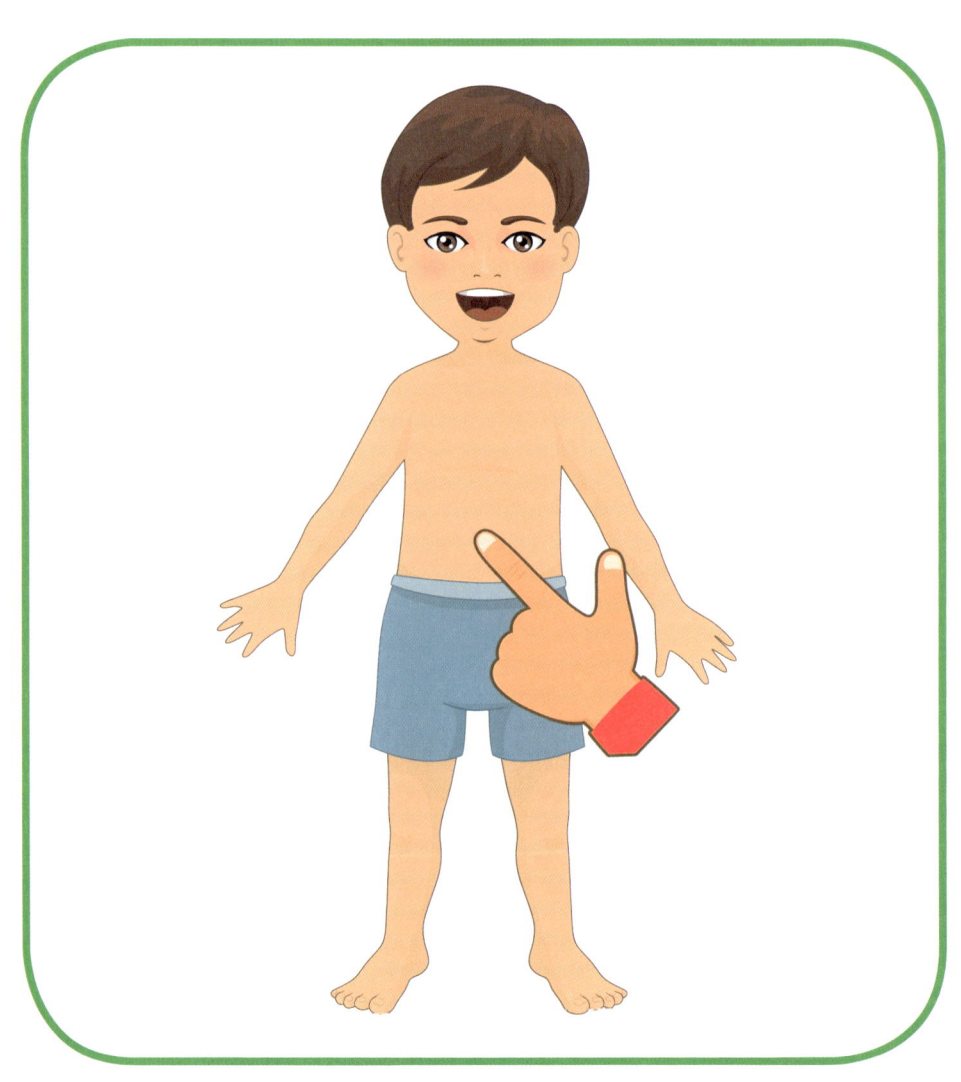

Can you touch your tummy?

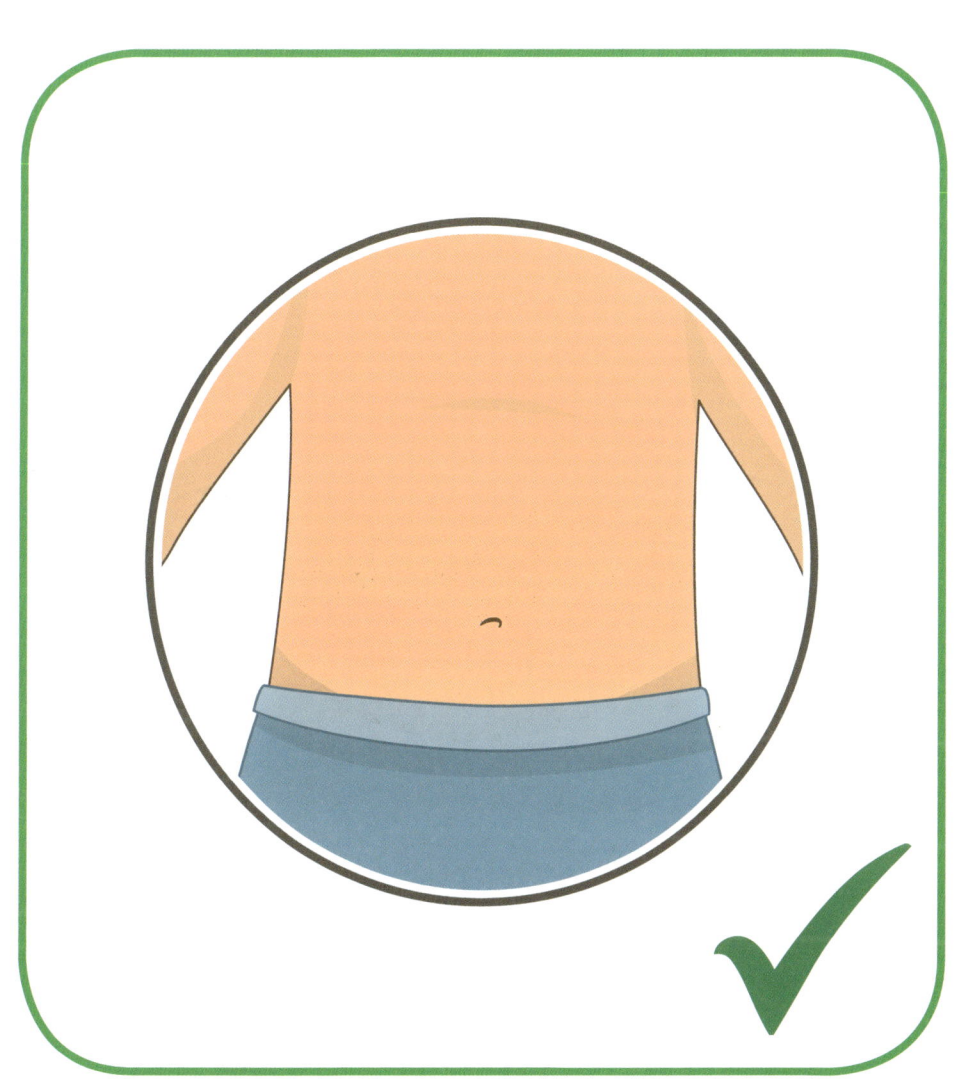

Yes, I can.

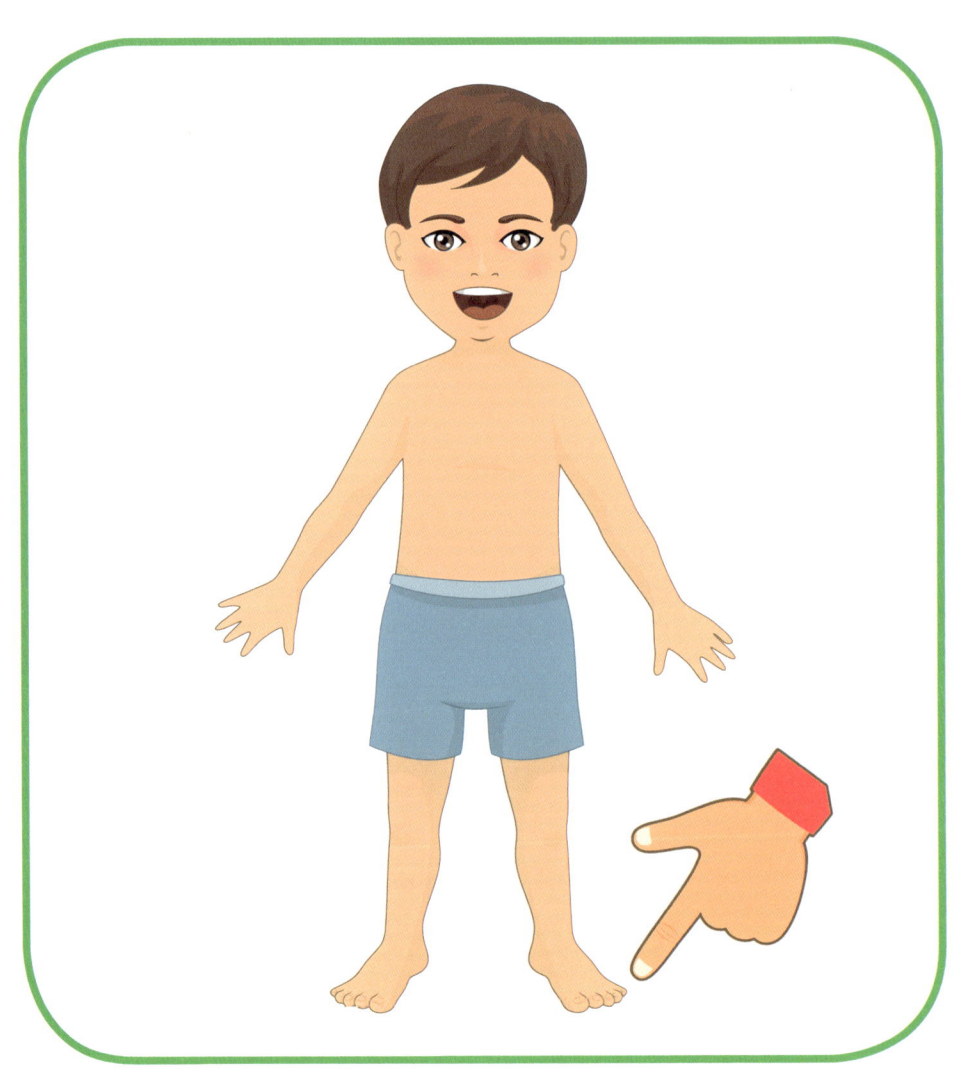

Can you touch
your toes?

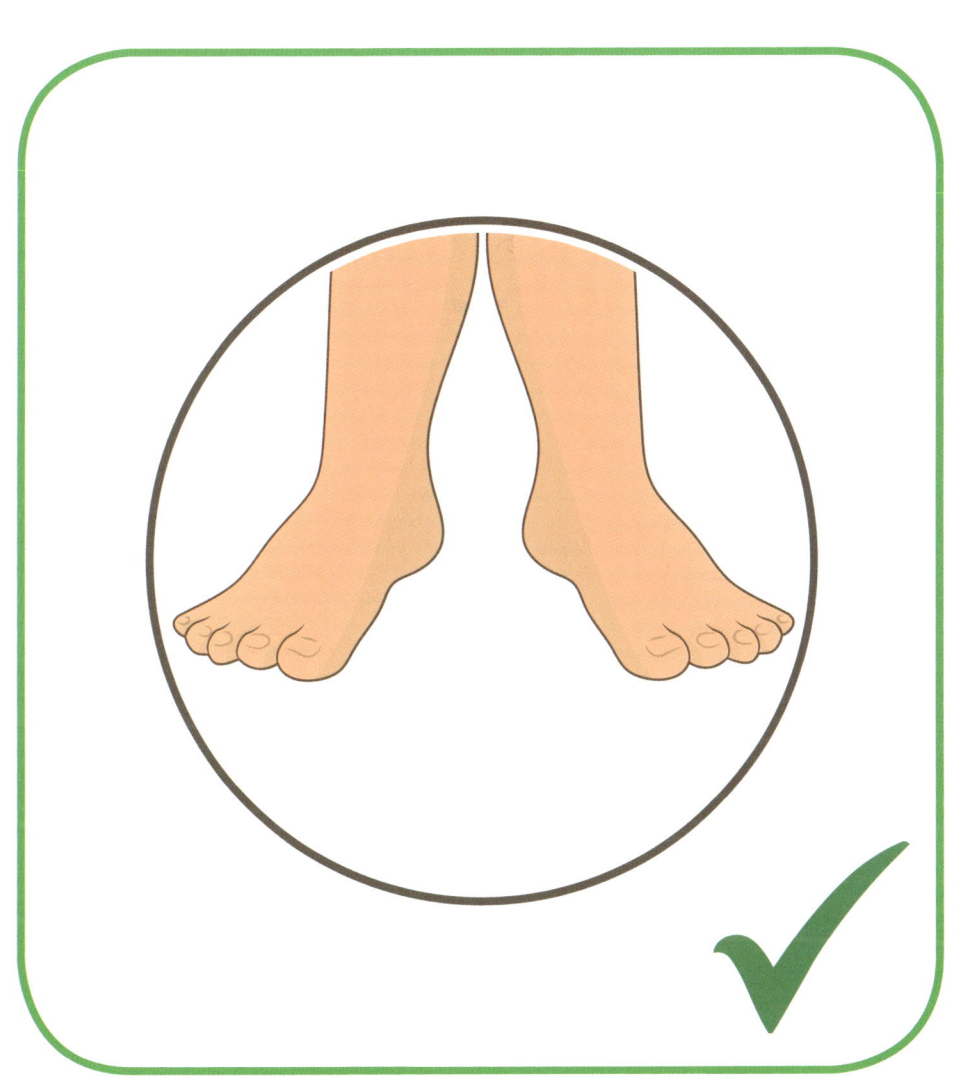

Yes, I can.

Let's learn more about the United Kingdom (UK).

Fish 'n' Chips